A Touch of His Freedom

Other Books in This Series

A Touch of His Freedom

MEDITATIONS ON FREEDOM IN CHRIST WITH ORIGINAL PHOTOS BY

CHARLES STANLEY

ZondervanPublishingHouse
Grand Rapids, Michigan

A Division of HarperCollins*Publishers*

A Touch of His Freedom
Copyright © 1991 by Charles Stanley

Requests for information should be addressed to:
Zondervan Publishing House
Grand Rapids, Michigan 49530

Library of Congress Cataloging-in-Publication Data

Stanley, Charles F.
    A touch of his freedom / by Charles Stanley.
        p. cm.
    ISBN 0-310-54620-6
    1. Freedom (Theology)—Meditations. I. Title.
BT810.2.S74   1991
233′.7—dc20   90–24872
                                                            CIP

All Scripture quotations, unless otherwise noted, are taken from the HOLY BIBLE: NEW INTERNATIONAL VERSION (North American Edition). Copyright © 1973, 1978, 1984, by the International Bible Society. Used by permission of Zondervan Bible Publishers.

Edited by Gerard Terpstra
Interior design and line illustrations by Art Jacobs

Printed in the United States of America

    96 / DH / 10 9 8 7 6 5

This edition is printed on acid-free paper and meets the American National Standards Institute Z39.48 standard.

Contents

Photographs

My deep appreciation to my son Andy for his able assistance in developing the manuscript and to my friend David Chamblee for his long hours with me in the darkroom.

Introduction

*F*or years my spiritual life was like a roller coaster, up and down, with far fewer ups than downs. I experienced more anxiety than peace, more fear than faith, more emptiness than fullness, and more failure than success.

Was I saved? Yes! Was I free? No! For all practical purposes my new-birth experience had not set me free. I knew the Lord's pardon, but not his freedom. Old habits still harassed me. Twisted emotions still paralyzed me. The power of sin continued to defeat me. Consequently, I knew no joy, only frustration. I longed for the freedom Jesus promised. But for some reason it always eluded my grasp.

My problem was not one of desire. I wished with all my heart to please God. But I was never able to follow through with any consistency. I always felt as if I were fighting a losing battle.

Eventually it dawned on me that I was in bondage; I was a prisoner. The reality of my situation pushed me to the brink of despair. I lived with an overwhelming sense of hopelessness and helplessness.

It was in the early morning hours, after crying out to the Lord throughout the night, that I suddenly realized that I must relinquish to him control of my entire life.

With a deep longing in my heart, I began to search the Scriptures with one objective—to know the joy of real freedom in Christ, freedom to become the person God intended me to be. And I found it. Jesus unlocked the door to my prison cell with six simple words: "The truth will set you free" (John 8:32).

With this promise in my heart I began to apply the principles that follow in this book. In doing so, I experienced a touch of freedom that transformed my life. I pray that God will use this book to expose areas of bondage in your life, and more important, that the truth will set *you* free.

A Touch of His Freedom

You will know the truth,
and the truth will set you free. . . .
So if the Son sets you free,
you will be free indeed.   John 8:32, 36

Truth That Sets Us Free

*T*ruth and freedom are constant companions. Where you find one, you will always find the other. Freedom in any area of life comes from discovering the truth about it. And discovering truth in a particular area always results in freedom of some kind.

It is when a child accepts the truth that there is nothing to be afraid of that she is finally free from a fear of the dark. It is only when a little boy accepts the truth that his father can and will catch him that he finds the freedom to leave the security of the diving board and jump into the pool. Likewise, it is only as we accept the truth of all that Christ did for us at Calvary that we will begin to enjoy the freedom he provided.

"The truth will set you free." In six simple words Jesus outlines the process by which any man, woman, boy, or girl can gain freedom in this life. Freedom is not gained through having our way or doing as we please. On the contrary, prisons are full of men and women who simply did as they pleased. These people certainly didn't gain freedom; they forfeited their freedom. And so it is with us every time we carelessly strike out on our own, to do our own thing. What results is not freedom, but bondage.

If I were to ask you whether or not you are free, you may be tempted to answer yes without giving it much thought. But let me ask you this, Are you constantly battling with fear, lust, jealousy, hatred, bitterness, conceit, deceitfulness, a lack of faith, or discouragement? Are there habits in your life over which you seem to have little or no control? Are there certain environments and people you avoid because of an insecurity you cannot overcome? If you answered yes to one or more of these questions, then you are not free. Don't be fooled by the fact that you are not in handcuffs or behind bars.

For the next thirty days we will focus on some specific areas of potential bondage as well as on the truth that provides the way to freedom. As the Holy Spirit brings areas of bondage in your life to the surface, spend some extra time meditating on those truths that correspond to your area of need. And in time, you will be "free indeed"!

Heavenly Father, thank you for providing me with a means by which I can be free. Thank you for paving the way through the death and resurrection of your Son. Now give me insight into your Word that I may uncover the liberating truths I so desperately need to make my freedom complete. And Father, don't let me get discouraged and quit before this journey is complete. Amen.

TOUCHSTONE

Where there is truth, there is freedom.

You must not eat from the tree
of the knowledge of good and evil,
for when you eat of it,
you will surely die. Genesis 2:17

Maximum Freedom

F or years I believed God was working against my personal freedom. I pictured him as a divine Lawgiver who spent the majority of his time creating new ways to further restrict my liberty. Statements such as the one found in Galatians 5:1 made little sense to me. I would read them over and over and wonder why, if Christ came to set us free, I felt like such a slave.

Then one day while I was reading the first three chapters of Genesis a thought popped into my mind: "Adam and Eve had only one rule." Imagine living in a world where there was only one rule! The implications are astounding. Most significant, however, is the fact that in the perfect environment, where God had everything just the way he wanted it, he issued only one "thou shalt not." To put it another way, God is not a God of rules. Our God is a God of freedom. In the beginning he placed the first man and woman in a beautiful garden and for all practical purposes said, "You are free to enjoy yourselves."

"So," you ask, "why all the moral and ethical taboos now? Whatever happened to the good old days of freedom?" The answer is found in Genesis 3. Our earliest ancestors did the very thing they were told not to do and so opened the door for sin to enter the world. And with sin came death. Thus mankind became a slave to sin and death.

Whereas our world teaches us that freedom is gained through throwing off all restraint, the Scriptures teach that the opposite is true. Human beings forfeited a great deal of their freedom in their attempt to gain absolute freedom. As we begin to put two and two together, it becomes increasingly clear that freedom is gained and maintained by adherence to God's laws. Just as a good father sets loving limitations for his children, so the heavenly Father sets moral and ethical perimeters for us.

Once again, the bottom line is trust. Can we trust that God knows what is best for us? Can we believe that he really has our best interests in mind? Adam and Eve didn't. And they lost the

very freedom they were convinced their sin would ensure them. What about you? Are you willing to accept the fact that God is a God of freedom—that his laws are for your protection, given to ensure, not hamper, your freedom? If so, take a few moments to surrender to God those areas over which you have maintained control. Confess your lack of faith. Now rest in the assurance that God will grant to you the maximum amount of freedom available in this sinful world.

Heavenly Father, thank you for loving me enough to set limits on what I may and may not do. Grant me the wisdom to stay within the confines you have so wisely established. By sending Christ to die you have assured me that you have my best interests in mind. I willingly surrender every area of my life with the assurance that in doing so I am guaranteed freedom. Amen.

TOUCHSTONE

*There is no greater freedom
than that found within the
confines of God's loving
limitations.*

Anyone who has died
has been freed from sin.   Romans 6:7

Dead Men Don't Sin

F reedom begins and ends at the cross of Christ. It was at Calvary that the penalty for our sin was dealt with once and for all. It was there that Christ was punished on our behalf in order that we might be free of sin's debt. But something else took place at the cross that equally effects our freedom. Not only was the penalty of sin dealt with that day, but the power of sin as well. Christ's death and resurrection marked the end of sin's power to control the believer. Just as sin could not control the Son of God, so it is powerless to control those who have been placed into Christ through faith.

Unfortunately, many who would nod in agreement with the above statement are anything but free experientially. They are still slaves to the same habits and sin that plagued them in their pre-Christian days. There is no victory over sin. There is little joy. Consequently, there is little reason to keep struggling. And so for many believers their motto becomes "Well, nobody's perfect."

God does not intend for us to continue to live as slaves to sin. The message of the cross is freedom from sin—both its penalty and its power. While it is true that we will always be temptable, it is not true that we must give in to temptation. The moment you were saved, you were given new life—Christ's life. You died to your old life; a life dominated by the power and lure of sin. Your new life is the same life that enabled Christ to walk this earth for thirty-three years without sinning. It is the very life that enabled him to walk out of the grave unaffected by death. On the day you were born again, you became a new person with a brand new potential in regard to sin and death.

To make this historical and theological truth a reality we must appropriate it. That is, we must accept it as fact and act on it. As long as we are convinced to the contrary, we will continue to live as slaves.

Have you acknowledged your freedom from sin's power?

Have you been claiming it? Or have you been relying on your feelings as indicators of your relationship to sin? Your feelings will tell you that nothing has changed; everything is as it has always been.

But God says you are different. He says you are dead to sin, and dead people are free from the power of sin. Who will you choose to believe today?

Heavenly Father, thank you for breaking the power of sin in my life. I want to experience this freedom you have made available. I accept the truth that I am free from sin's power. I am dead to sin and alive to you. I claim ahead of time the victory that is mine in Christ. Remind me of this precious truth as I face the battles this day brings. Amen.

TOUCHSTONE

*We are as free as we dare to
believe ourselves to be.*

*Do not conform any longer
to the pattern of this world,
but be transformed by the renewing
of your mind.   Romans 12:2*

Transformed!

*M*ost of us have had the frustrating experience of making a sincere commitment only to find that several days later we have abandoned it. I call it the *youth-camp syndrome*. As a teenager I attended church camp just about every summer. As is the case with many camps, we always ended the week with a commitment service. Every year was the same. Everybody cried and promised God the moon—no more lying, cursing, cheating, smoking, drinking, and on and on it went. Unfortunately, most of those promises were broken before we made it back to the church parking lot the next afternoon!

I believe most of the decisions made during those sessions were sincere. The problem was that no one taught us how to follow through. We were clear on the *oughts* and *ought nots*. It was the *how tos* that remained a mystery. Year after year, that one crucial element managed to get left out of those otherwise excellent messages. And consequently, it was left out of our lives as well.

Because of his background, the apostle Paul knew all too well the frustration of knowing what to do without knowing how to do it. No doubt it was his own experience that made him sensitive to his readers' needs in this area. And so in one perfectly penned statement he summarized the key to consistent change: "by the renewing of your mind."

Paul knew that our behavior is directly affected by the way we think. For real change to take place externally, there must first be a change in our thinking. Until we get involved in the process of renewing our minds, any behavioral change is going to be short-lived.

Renewing the mind is a little like refinishing furniture. It is a two-stage process. It involves taking off the old and replacing it with the new. The old is the lies you have learned to tell or were taught by those around you; it is the attitudes and ideas that have become a part of your thinking but do not reflect reality. The

new is the truth. To renew your mind is to involve yourself in the process of allowing God to bring to the surface the lies you have mistakenly accepted and replace them with truth. To the degree that you do this, your behavior will be transformed. The remainder of this book is designed to aid you in this life-changing process.

Heavenly Father, thank you for giving me insight into how I am to go about making the principles of your Word a daily reality in my life. Thank you for not expecting instant change. As I open your Word, guide me to those portions of Scripture that contain the specific truths that I need for renewing my mind today. Thank you for providing such a simple way to ensure my freedom from the world and its destructive influence. Amen.

TOUCHSTONE

*Biblical imperatives, apart
from biblical thinking,
result in short-term
obedience and long-term
frustration.*

Therefore, there is now no condemnation for those who are in Christ Jesus, because through Christ Jesus the law of the Spirit of life set me free from the law of sin and death. Romans 8:1

No Condemnation

*D*o you believe God likes you? "Don't you mean, 'loves me'?" you ask. No, *likes* you. Do you believe God likes you? This is one of my favorite questions. The reason is that it cuts through to the core of how an individual really believes God feels about him or her. So, do you think God likes you? If he were to show up in bodily form, do you think he would seek you out? Would you be someone he would enjoy being around?

Isn't it strange how much more comfortable we are with the concept of *love* than with the concept of *like* when it comes to God's feelings toward us? Why do you think that is true? Often the reason lies in the fact that we have not come to grips with the real extent to which God has forgiven us. Consequently, we live with a subtle sense of condemnation. It's as if there is always a dark cloud separating us from God. We say we are forgiven, but in our hearts we are never fully convinced that God isn't still a little angry with us.

The truth is, every reason God had for being angry with us was dealt with at Calvary. Our forgiveness is so complete that God is not only free to love us, he can like us as well. Think about this: "There is now no condemnation for those who are in Christ Jesus." If you have placed your trust in Christ for the forgiveness of your sins, the Bible says you are positionally in Christ. And once you were placed into Christ, you were separated from the guilt that once brought divine condemnation. You are not condemned. Christ was condemned on your behalf, and now you are free!

"But," you ask, "why do I feel so condemned? Why don't I feel forgiven?" It's probably because you have not made up your mind to take God at his word. Instead, you have measured your worthiness and acceptability by your performance. To be free from feelings of condemnation you must renew your mind to this powerful truth: "There is *now* no condemnation for those who are in Christ Jesus."

Heavenly Father, thank you for desiring a relationship with me so intensely that you were willing to remove all the obstacles standing in the way. Give me the courage to ignore my feelings and take you at your word. By faith I choose to accept right now the fact that I am not condemned. In Jesus' name. Amen.

TOUCHSTONE

*In Christ we are completely
free from all condemnation.*

In love he predestined us to be adopted
as his sons through Jesus Christ,
in accordance with his pleasure and will.

Ephesians 1:5

How Free Is Free?

T here is all the difference in the world between working *to gain* someone's acceptance and working *because of* some-one's acceptance. I meet people all the time who feel compelled to serve God in order to merit his love and acceptance. Often this is the result of a theological error they have been taught since childhood. "You better be good or else. . . ." On other occasions it stems from growing up in a home where parental acceptance depended on their behavior. "Be a good girl, and daddy will love you." This pattern of thinking can become so entrenched that adults will work themselves into the grave in an attempt to prove to their parents that they were not a failure. I have met men who were driven by a desire to gain their father's approval long after their father had passed away!

When this system of performance-based acceptance is transferred to our heavenly Father, the result is legalism. Legalism is an attitude. It is a system of thinking in which an individual attempts to gain God's love and acceptance through good works or service. Some people sincerely believe their salvation is at stake. For others it is a vague feeling of divine disapproval of which they are trying to rid themselves. Either way, however, legalism always leads to the same dead end: a lack of joy, a critical spirit, and an inability to be transparent.

Freedom from legalism comes through accepting the truth about our favored position in the family of God. Those who have put their trust in Christ have been *adopted* into his family. There is no concept that speaks any clearer of acceptance than adoption. Whereas a pregnancy can come as a surprise, adoption is always something that is premeditated and planned. While you and I were still without hope, God set the stage to adopt us into his family (Rom. 5:8).

Do you feel that you must work in order to gain God's acceptance? Do you find yourself being critical of those who do not serve the Lord with the same fervor as you? Have you

developed a martyr's attitude toward your service for the Lord? If you answered yes to any of these questions, it could be that you are not really resting in the finished work of Christ—a work that settled the question of your acceptability once and for all, a work that provided you with an eternal place in the family of God, a work that allows you to call the God of the universe your Father!

Heavenly Father, you are the God who overcame the barrier sin had put between us. Thank you for seeking me out and adopting me into your family. Thank you that I don't have to serve you in order to earn your love and acceptance. Remind me often of this liberating truth. Renew my mind so that I may serve you out of a heart of gratitude and joy. Amen.

TOUCHSTONE

God's unconditional acceptance sets us free to serve him with unending joy.

You intended to harm me,
but God intended it for good
to accomplish what is now being done. . . .
Genesis 50:20

Free to Believe

*T*rusting God to use the circumstantial disappointments in life is difficult. Trusting him to work through people's evil intentions is something else entirely. It is one thing when the church picnic is rained out. It is quite another when a "friend" at work intentionally lies in order to get your job.

When events such as a betrayal occur, a wall of frustration clouds our relationship with God. We ask, "Why didn't you stop this? Didn't you know this was going to happen?" As our frustration turns to doubt, we lose confidence in God's concern and involvement in our lives. After all, if he really has our best interest in mind, why would he allow us to suffer at the hands of our adversaries?

To be free from the doubt and resentment we tend to feel toward God when we are intentionally hurt by others, we must focus on the principle stated so clearly by Joseph: "You intended to harm me, but God intended it for good. . . ." Through all the rejection and abuse Joseph encountered at the hands of his brothers, God had not abandoned him. Just the opposite was true. Through the intentional mistreatment Joseph experienced, God was working to accomplish his divine plan.

There is a catch. In order for God to turn a negative situation into a positive one, we must remain faithful through the process. Imagine what would have happened if Joseph had allowed himself to grow bitter at God and at his family. This story may not have had such a happy ending. It was Joseph's faithfulness through the process that gave God the freedom to work.

Have you been mistreated? Has your faith in God's goodness and sovereignty been shaken? Are you willing to begin renewing your mind to the truth that what people may have intended for evil, God can use for your good and his glory?

Heavenly Father, you are the God who sovereignly uses even the intentional evil of human beings to carry out your will. Forgive me for harboring anger toward you for the wrongs done to me by others. I choose to believe that you are intimately aquainted with every detail of my life, that nothing goes unnoticed. Thank you for the assurance I have through Christ. I am excited to see how you will demonstrate your faithfulness in the days and weeks ahead. Amen.

TOUCHSTONE

*The evil intentions of people,
when responded to correctly,
can become the very means
by which God carries out
his divine plans.*

But immediately Jesus said to them:
"Take courage! It is I. Don't be afraid."
                                    Matthew 14:27

Fear Not!

F ear is probably the number-one cause of paralysis. By paralysis I do not mean some physical malady. The paralysis caused by fear affects the mind, will, and emotions. It is paralysis of the soul.

For years I have lived with the fear of being left alone. My father died when I was a baby. My mother worked in a mill while I was growing up. She had to leave for work while I was still asleep. It seemed as if I was always being left alone. As is always the case with unpleasant early experiences, mine also left their mark.

All of us have fears. Many have a fear of failure. Others struggle with a fear of commitment or of finding themselves trapped in a relationship. Occasionally I talk with a young person who fears growing old. And if we are honest, we have all felt a twinge of fear at the thought of dying.

As the disciples peered out across the windswept sea, they saw what they thought to be a ghost. The Scripture tells us that these brave, seasoned sailors actually "cried out" in fear (Matt. 14:26). Their fears were short-lived, however, for the next sound they heard was the voice of Jesus. And his presence alone brought peace to their hearts while the sea continued to rage around them.

Those who have placed their trust in Christ as Savior are never required to face either the known or the unknown alone; he is there. In those times when our fear surges from our knowledge of what is to come, he is there. He understands the terror that accompanies the prospect of severe pain, the loss of a loved one, or death. The Savior is no stranger to these. In times when it is the unknown that causes us to fear, he is there. He is there with full knowledge of what is to come and with the grace to sustain us.

Have your fears become a controlling force in your life? Do you find yourself missing opportunities and experiences because

of your fear of failure, rejection, or the future in general? God never intended for you to be controlled by fear. He is, however, willing to use your fears to move you to a place of greater dependence on him. Whatever it is you are facing, remember, he is there.

Heavenly Father, thank you for sending a Savior who can identify with my fears and who promised his presence in the midst of both the known and the unknown. Grant me the wisdom to draw upon his grace when I am overcome by fear. May my courage bring honor and glory to your name. Amen.

TOUCHSTONE

As you walk through the valley of the unknown, you will find the footprints of Jesus both in front of you and beside you.

Who is this uncircumcised Philistine
that he should defy the armies
of the living God?   1 Samuel 17:26

Overcoming Obstacles

D ay after day the army of Israel stood paralyzed with fear. However, it wasn't the size or strength of the Philistine army that terrified them. Israel had been outnumbered before. This time it was different. This time it was one soldier who stood between Israel and victory. Only one soldier. But he was no ordinary soldier. This was Goliath, the champion of the Philistine army—a warrior so intimidating to look upon that even his blasphemous taunts could not anger a single Israelite soldier to the point of being willing to confront him. To challenge Goliath would mean certain death. Or so it seemed.

Enter David. Upon seeing and hearing Goliath, the young shepherd asked a very insightful question—a question that introduced a fresh new perspective to the scene: "Who is this uncircumcised Philistine that he should defy the armies of the living God?"

Everyone saw the same towering figure in the valley. They all heard the same profanities. But David interpreted these things differently from those around him. Saul and his men saw Goliath as *their* enemy. David, on the other hand, saw Goliath as one coming against the living God. Take a moment and read David's speech beginning in 1 Samuel 17:45.

We all face Goliaths from time to time. Perhaps they are circumstances at work, relationships at home, or decisions just too big for us to handle. Like the soldiers of Israel, we are often overwhelmed with our own sense of inadequacy. So we stand motionless, lacking the courage to move ahead.

Freedom comes as we develop young David's attitude, when we adopt a heavenly perspective on all of life's obstacles. Because we are children of the living God, anything that comes against us must come through him. And in the words of the apostle Paul, "If God is for us, who can be against us?" (Rom. 8:31).

As you contemplate the challenges of today, don't make the mistake of measuring your potential success by your ability or

past performance. To do so means instant insecurity and discouragement. God gains much greater honor through our *availability* than through our *ability*. He does not expect you to work out the details of how everything is going to come together today. All he requires is that you show up and do what you believe he wants you to do, trusting him to fill in the gaps.

Heavenly Father, thank you for allowing me to face what seem to be impossible obstacles. These obstacles serve as a constant reminder of my intense dependence on you. Thank you as well for the promise of your strength and sufficiency. It is a great comfort to know I do not face Goliath alone. Father, I am available. I am trusting you to make me able. Amen.

TOUCHSTONE

God is not nearly so interested in your ability *as he is in your* availability.

Be kind and compassionate to one another,
forgiving each other,
just as in Christ God forgave you.   Ephesians 4:32

Freedom to Forgive

*I*f you are like most people, you have been hurt at some time in your life. You may have suffered intense rejection as a child or at this very moment you may be in a relationship that results in a daily dose of hurt. Hurt, regardless of its intensity or longevity, sets each of us up to become a slave to resentment and bitterness. Our natural tendency is to hold on to the wrongs done to us by others. Without realizing it, we begin to view those who have offended us as owing us something. We begin expecting them to somehow pay us back for the emotional stress they have brought to our lives. Our desire to get even often results in fantasies of conversations we would like to have and plans we wish we had the nerve to carry out.

This is one of the most damaging types of bondage. I have watched men and women destroy those whom they loved the most because of their refusal to deal with resentment. Resentment is like a poisoned fountain. It pours out its poison into every relationship. Consequently, husbands, wives, children, and employees who had nothing to do with causing the hurt become its victims.

There is a way out. It is actually very simple. Forgive. "That's impossible," you say. Oh really? Think about it; what makes it impossible? Really only one thing, your refusal to let go of the lie that somehow those who have wronged you owe you something. To forgive is simply to mentally release the offending party of any obligation. "But," you say, "you don't know the pain and trouble they have caused me." That is true. But think about the pain and sorrow they are continuing to cause you by your refusal to let go. When you weigh the temporary joy you may experience when you contemplate revenge against the negative fallout in your relationships with others, is it worth it?

When it comes to forgiveness, Jesus set the standard. Meditate for a moment on this thought: *He who had the greatest reason not to forgive paid the highest price in order to forgive.* Jesus

died in order to make it *possible* for him to forgive you; and then, having paved the way, he *forgave* you. For us, forgiveness is simply a mental decision. For Christ, it was a matter of life and death. He chose death, in order that you may have life. Now then, if Christ was willing to release you from the debt you owed him, who are you to refuse to release those who have offended you? Besides, what do you have to gain by continuing to cling to your hurt? Why not let go of it right now?

Heavenly Father, you are the God who forgives. Thank you for forgiving me. Bring to my mind those wrongs I continue to cling to. Give me the strength and courage to forgive, as you have so graciously forgiven me. Amen.

TOUCHSTONE

*He who had the greatest
reason not to forgive paid
the highest price in order to
forgive.*

Then Peter came to Jesus and asked, "Lord, how many times shall I forgive my brother when he sins against me? Up to seven times?"
Jesus answered, "I tell you, not seven times, but seventy-seven times." Matthew 18:21–22

... and Forgive and Forgive and Forgive

*A*ll of us have been told at some time to *forgive and forget*. It sure sounds like a good idea, but unfortunately it is impossible to do. We do not have the ability to erase our memory banks. But wouldn't it be great if we could? Every time someone threw a hurtful remark your way, you could forgive that person and forget the wrong right there on the spot. The next time you saw him you wouldn't have anything to hold against him; it would have been forgotten. Such a system would make the forgiveness process so much easier. Forgiving someone for a one-time offense is not nearly so difficult as forgiving someone who is constantly hurting you. No doubt it was this very dilemma that drove Peter to ask Jesus how many times he should forgive his brother. Peter thought seven times was a gracious plenty. Jesus countered by suggesting seventy-seven times. From the parable that follows it is clear that Jesus really meant for Peter to forgive his brother every time he sinned against him— regardless of how often the occasion arose.

If you are like many people, there is someone in your life who hurts or offends you almost daily. It may be your unsaved spouse. It could be one of your children. For many it is an employee or an employer. Whatever the case, if there is someone like that in your life, you run a constant risk of becoming bitter. Simply forgiving such a person one time is not enough. You may literally have to forgive him seven times a day. In some extreme cases you may have to forgive him every time he opens his mouth!

I frequently talk to people who are harboring anger and resentment. When I raise the forgiveness issue, they will often respond by saying, "I have forgiven them, but they keep on hurting me!" Somewhere along the way these people got the idea

that once they forgive the offending party, that should be the end of it. But that is rarely the case. As long as an individual continues to offend, you must continue to forgive. That is, you must right there on the spot mentally release the offending person of any obligation. When I am in that kind of situation, I just smile and under my breath whisper, "Lord, I forgive her just as you forgave me."

The only way to stay free from resentment and bitterness is to get into the habit of forgiving immediately and unconditionally. Don't put it off. Delay gives the Enemy time to work on you. Think about it, how many times has God had to forgive you for the same sin? How many times has he had to forgive you for the same thing more than once on the same day? Follow his example—forgive and . . . well, just forgive.

Heavenly Father, you are the God whose forgiveness knows no boundaries. Just as you are constantly forgiving me, give me the wisdom to do the same for others. And in this way keep me free from the web of bitterness. Amen.

TOUCHSTONE

*Forgive completely,
immediately,* and
unconditionally.

And will not God bring about justice for his chosen ones, who cry out to him day and night? Will he keep putting them off? Luke 18:7

Justice for All

We have all been treated unjustly at some time in our life. Our first impulse is to retaliate, to strike back, to work out a way to get even. To be honest, when I see people mistreated, I am often tempted to take revenge on their behalf. It is hard to sit by and watch others being taken advantage of—especially when it so often appears that the offending party goes unpunished.

The truth is that God is keeping good records of the injustice in this world. No evil act goes unnoticed. From snatched purses to lawsuits to abused children, he sees them all and takes careful notes. One day the last trumpet will sound and life as we know it will end. At that time the Judge of this world will set up court. Every crime since the beginning of time will be tried. And the amazing thing is that the Judge will also serve as an eyewitness to every case! When all is said and done, every man and woman will receive retribution of some kind for his or her deeds done on earth (2 Cor. 5:10).

The key to being set free from a desire to return evil for evil is to keep in mind two important truths. First, you are not the Judge, Christ is. He will return as the Judge of all mankind and dole out justice according to his infinite wisdom and knowledge. Second, the Son of God is still waiting to be avenged for the wrong done to him. As badly as you may have been mistreated, remember that Christ did not take revenge on those who crucified him. He reserved that for a future date. And so we wait. But we wait knowing that in the end all wrongs will be made right. And not one unjust act will have gone unnoticed.

Have you been treated unfairly? Are you guilty of attempting to get revenge through your words, your refusal to do your best for someone, or some other form of retribution? If so, are you now willing to turn that responsibility over to its rightful owner?

Heavenly Father, you are a God of justice—a God who allows no unjust deed to escape your notice. Thank you for the promise of retribution. Give us the courage to trust you. And grant us the self-control to wait. Amen.

TOUCHSTONE

*The day of judgment will be
a day of justice.*

What causes fights and quarrels among you? Don't they come from your desires that battle within you? You want something but don't get it. You kill and covet, but you cannot have what you want. You quarrel and fight.

James 4:1

When Rights Become Wrongs

*W*hat at first appears to be a serious case of oversimplification is actually a penetrating truth. All of our relational conflicts stem from our pursuit of pleasure or satisfaction. Since the fulfillment of our desires is often viewed as an infringement on the rights and fulfillment of others, there is conflict. And so husbands fight with their wives over where to spend their vacation. Employees and employers argue over wage increases. Neighbors argue over property lines. Think about your last confrontation. How did it begin? Isn't it true that it ultimately stemmed from someone's desire to have his or her own way?

When James speaks of desires, he is referring to every sort of desire—both good and evil. It is our desires that determine the arena for the conflicts we encounter. To make matters worse, we live in a society that exonerates those who know how to get their way. Yet it is that very characteristic that often serves as the basis for one's inability to get along with others.

As Christians we have been called to live beyond the world's standards. Specifically, we are not to live life consumed by having our way. Freedom from this treadmill pursuit of pleasure comes through the most basic of all Christian principles—trust. When it appears that your needs are about to go unmet and that your desires are going to go unfulfilled, your response must be, "Lord, I trust you." To do otherwise is to set yourself up for conflict. The apostle Paul knew what it was like to go without. Drawing from the wealth of his own experience, he encouraged a group of needy believers with these words: "My God will meet all your needs according to his glorious riches in Christ Jesus" (Phil. 4:19).

What is the source of your quarrels? God says that ultimately

it is your determination to have your way. Today begin surrendering your rights and desires to the One who has promised to meet your every need. One practical way is to write down the areas of conflict in your life. Beside each one write down the right or desire that contributes to your run-ins. One by one surrender those to God. Then place your list in an envelope and put it somewhere as a reminder that you are trusting God to meet your every need—his way and in his time.

Heavenly Father, you are the God who is intimately aquainted with my every need and desire. Thank you for concerning yourself with the details of my life. Thank you for the example I have in Christ, who willingly laid down his rights—even his right to life itself. Give me the courage to trust you when others prove insensitive and untrustworthy. Amen.

TOUCHSTONE

Life's conflicts diminish as we surrender our rights and desires to Christ.

Let us then approach the throne of grace
    with confidence,
so that we may receive mercy and find grace
to help us in our time of need.   Hebrews 4:16

Great Expectations

A nyone who has experienced the frustration of unanswered prayer knows what it is like to be disappointed with God. When he does not respond the way we expect him to, we immediately begin searching for the reason. The age-old questions concerning God and evil begin to whirl through our minds: "If God is a good God why would he allow. . . ? If God is all powerful, surely he could have stopped. . . ." And each round of questions steadily chips away at our confidence. For many, this process leads to total hopelessness and despair. For others, it culminates in faith so crippled that this faith becomes virtually useless.

I too have been disappointed with God. My experiences have brought me to these two conclusions: (1) God always keeps his promises, but (2) we are not always careful to claim just his promises. Often we confuse what he has promised with what we wish, desire, and hope for. Consequently, our faith becomes focused on the fulfillment of things God never intended to do. And we are disappointed.

Nowhere in Scripture does God promise to fine-tune our circumstances to our liking. Nowhere does he guarantee a pain-free, problem-free environment. As his children we are free to ask for whatever our hearts desire. But as his servants we must submit ourselves to his sovereign will.

There are, however, two promised gifts we can claim with absolute confidence—mercy and grace. The Savior can sympathize with you. He knows from experience what it means to suffer alone. When you cry out to him, he moves to the edge of his throne to listen attentively and compassionately. You hold a tender place in his heart.

But he does more than listen. Jesus personally extends to us the strength we need to endure whatever it is we are facing. That is the idea behind the term *grace*.

The heavenly Father may elect not to change the nature of

your circumstances. He may in fact choose to deliver you *through* hard times rather than *from* them. His answer to your prayers of deliverance may be "Hang in there!" But this is no time for disappointment. God is not ignoring your cry for help; he is extending to you the power to withstand whatever difficulty or pain life brings your way. And he does so in the hope that having withstood it, you will one day stand and give him all the glory!

Heavenly Father, thank you for not turning a deaf ear to the cries of your children. Father, I confess that I have been disappointed with what has seemed to be a lack of concern on your part. I realize now that I was holding you to promises you never made. As I face the difficulties of life I do so with the confidence that you listen to my cries compassionately and that you will always provide me with the strength to endure. Amen.

TOUCHSTONE

*When you come to the Father,
you will always find mercy
and grace in time of need.*

Who are you to judge someone else's servant?
To his own master he stands or falls.
And he will stand. . . . Romans 14:4

Agree to Disagree

*T*here are issues on which the church of the Lord Jesus will never come to full agreement. The apostle Paul coined the term "disputable matters" when referring to these types of things. In his day the hot topic was eating meat offered to idols or not eating meat at all. Today believers debate over things such as clapping in church, music, dancing, hair style, drinking wine, and the proper form of church government.

As important as these things may be, God never intended for them to divide the church. Yet it is amazing how they cause believers to become highly critical of one another. This attitude results in gossip, slander, divisiveness, and many other evils that the Scripture clearly teaches are wrong (Eph. 4:29–32). Those who involve themselves in this type of criticism are good examples of what Jesus was referring to when he said, "Why do you look at the speck of sawdust in your brother's eye and pay no attention to the plank in your own eye?" (Matt. 7:3)

The truth that sets us free from a critical spirit is found in Romans 14. Paul makes it penetratingly clear that we have no right to judge someone else's servant. What he is referring to is the fact that each of us is a servant of Christ. And the time will come when each of us will give an account of our life to him— the One to whom we are ultimately accountable. When it comes to disputable matters, we were never appointed to be one another's judge. We are free to disagree, but we are never free to criticize. To judge others for their opinion on "disputable matters" is to take upon ourselves a role God reserves exclusively for his Son.

Do you find yourself criticizing other believers for things that are really matters of opinion rather than clear moral or ethical issues? Do you tend to judge others' spirituality, based on trivial things? Are you guilty of taking upon yourself the role of judge?

Heavenly Father, you are the judge of the living and the dead. You are the God who is able to see beyond a person's actions and take into account the motivation of his heart. I am grateful that you have reserved for yourself the role of judge. Thank you for not setting me as a judge over my brothers and sisters in Christ in the area of disputable matters. Please convict me when I become critical and thus take upon myself a responsibility you never intended for me. Thank you for the freedom and diversity that there is in the body of Christ. Amen.

TOUCHSTONE

*To our own Master we will
stand or fall.*

*And I hope that, as you have understood us in part,
you will come to understand fully
that you can boast of us just as we will boast of you
in the day of the Lord Jesus.   2 Corinthians 1:14*

Beyond Behavior

*W*e all know people we don't like. It's the guy you pretend not to see as he waves to you across the parking lot. It's the "old friend" whose calls your secretary knows not to put through to your office. It's the self-styled theologian who always wants to talk to you after church. It's an employee, an employer, a neighbor, a relative. . . . The list goes on and on. They are everywhere.

I know, I know—Christians are supposed to love everybody. That may be true. But *love* is one thing, *like* is something else altogether. We can force ourselves to be kind and patient and gentle and all of that. But how do you make yourself *like* someone?

To overcome our dislike for people we must first understand a little bit about what makes them tick. Folks are not generally born unlikable. They get that way with time and abuse. As we begin to understand the person behind the behavior, some of the walls begin to come down.

God used an event several summers ago to remind me once again of this simple yet profound principle. The incident took place at a family-life conference where I was the keynote speaker. Early in the week I had my first encounter with Jimmy. Actually, I heard him before I saw him. We were just about to begin a session when a raspy voice could be heard practically screaming, "Excuse me. Excuse me." Through a crowd came this little boy, dragging a chair behind him. After almost knocking down several attendees, he made his way to the front, crammed his chair between two other chairs—both of which were occupied— and sat down. He looked around for a second, stood up, and started yelling back over the crowd, "Mom, Mom, there's a seat up here!" My first impulse was to snatch him up and tan his hide. By mid-week everybody knew Jimmy—and shared my sentiments.

Then something interesting happened. A woman at the

conference pulled me over to the side to tell me something in private. She asked if I had met Jimmy yet. I smiled and assured her I had. She explained how she had befriended him early in the week and that they had been talking together. She continued, "This morning Jimmy walked up and said he had something he wanted to tell me. I asked him what it was. Without hesitation he said, 'My daddy dropped dead in January, and I'm having a hard time.'" When I heard that, my feelings for Jimmy immediately changed. I wanted to find him and hug him. Now I understood.

Who is it that just drives you crazy? You will be free from many of your negative feelings when you discover the truth about the person behind the behavior.

Heavenly Father, thank you for looking beyond my behavior and loving me anyway. Grant me the wisdom and the courage to do the same for others. As I encounter those whose company I don't particularly enjoy, remind me to look at the person behind the behavior. Amen.

TOUCHSTONE

*Take time to look at the
person behind the behavior.*

*I tell you, use worldly wealth to gain friends
for yourselves, so that when it is gone,
you will be welcomed into eternal dwellings.*

Luke 16:9

Financial Freedom

*E*ven a casual look around is enough to confirm the truth of these words that Paul wrote to Timothy: "The love of money is a root of all kinds of evil" (1 Tim. 6:10). Volumes could be written on the ways this truth has worked its way into the lives of unsuspecting men and women. Every crime has at some time been motivated by somebody's all-consuming desire for money. On a more personal level, the love of money has been the wedge used to alienate husbands from wives, fathers from sons, and even best friends from each other. The greatest tragedies, however, are those in which a man or woman's love for money has caused him or her to drift away from Christ.

What makes this such a tough issue is that it is difficult to discern whether or not we are victims of this dreaded infirmity. How can we tell if we are lovers of money? Rather than give us a list of things by which to evaluate ourselves, Jesus offered us a new perspective on the whole issue of our finances. The implication is that if we will adopt his attitude toward money, we will never have to worry about its becoming the object of our affection.

For some, money is an end in itself. Christ viewed it as a means to an end. Specifically, he viewed it as *a temporal means to an eternal end*. God views every dollar we possess as well as all our material possessions as tools—tools to be used with the express purpose of bringing people into his kingdom. Take a minute and read Jesus' parable in Luke 16. Take careful note of verse 9. Jesus said that when we enter heaven, we will be greeted by those whose salvation was secured by our giving. Every dollar you send to missions that is instrumental in someone's coming to Christ will add one more person to your welcoming party.

When you think about your money, you are to think of it in this light: "How can I use what I own to more effectively reach people for Christ?" To the degree that you adopt this attitude

toward your money and possessions, you will be free from the love of money.

Heavenly Father, you are the God who takes what is temporal and uses it to bring yourself eternal glory. Thank you for those who gave of their time and energy and possessions to provide me with an opportunity to hear the gospel. Remind me of this truth daily. And in doing so, protect me from setting my affection on the accumulation of wealth. Amen.

TOUCHSTONE

Money is a means, not an end—a tool to provide people with opportunities to hear and accept the gospel of Christ.

When they came to the border of Mysia,
they tried to enter Bithynia,
but the Spirit of Jesus would not allow them to.
                                        Acts 16:7 (cf. Jeremiah 29:11)

Future Frustrations

O ne of the most common questions I am asked is, "How can I know God's will for my life?" Many times there is a great deal of anxiety in the voice of the one asking. Understandably so. It is discouraging when we don't know what direction God wants us to take.

It is unfortunate that so many Christians are paralyzed by the question of God's will. Many feel that until they know absolutely, beyond a shadow of a doubt, exactly what God wants them to do, they don't dare to make a move. But that is not the model we find in Scripture. In fact just the opposite is true.

Paul is a good example. He knew God's general will for his life—that he should preach the gospel. So he took off to do just that. The implication of what happened in Acts 16 is that Paul did not always get specific direction from the Lord. And when he didn't, he simply did what he thought was best for him to do. Apparently Paul heard that Bithynia needed the gospel; so he headed out in that direction. But God had another plan for Paul and blocked the way.

If you don't know God's specific will for your life, chances are it is because he has not revealed it to you. In the meantime you are free to begin moving in whatever direction you feel is appropriate. If you make a wrong choice, God will stop you just as he stopped the apostle Paul. God never intended for us to be paralyzed by his silence. There is enough general guidance in his Word to get us on our way. As long as we are unsure of the specifics in life, we are free to make what we consider the best decision to be—again, knowing that he can step in at any time and change our direction.

Has your search for the "perfect" will of God left you in a holding pattern? Maybe it's time to make a move. Don't be afraid to do what you feel is best. For within the plan God has designed for each of us, he has included a measure of freedom as well.

Heavenly Father, you are the God who knows my fears and frustrations concerning the future. I confess that often I get anxious about your timing. Beginning today I am choosing to trust you to reveal everything I need to know at the perfect time. For now I will do what I feel is best. Through this process I am trusting you to stop me should I begin to move in the wrong direction or in the right direction at the wrong time. Thank you for the freedom to think and decide for myself as well as for your promise of guidance. Lead me to a perfect balance of the two. Amen.

TOUCHSTONE

Included in God's will for your life is the freedom to explore and pursue the desires of your heart.

Let us not become weary in doing good,
for at the proper time we will reap a harvest
if we do not give up.   Galatians 6:9

Dealing With Discouragement

E veryone enjoys immediate results. Whether it is a sales-man making calls, a grandmother planting a garden, or a college graduate sending out resumés—no one enjoys waiting. This same tendency carries over into our spiritual lives as well. Once we commit a situation to the Lord, we expect things to change—*now!* If we are convicted of a particular sin in our lives and turn to our heavenly Father for help, we want to experience instantaneous freedom. When we become burdened for someone and begin praying on that person's behalf, we expect God to do something soon.

But often nothing happens. Our prayers go unanswered, and our effort goes unrewarded. It is during these times that we are most prone to get discouraged. Our confidence in the faithfulness of God wanes. We may even entertain doubts about his very existence.

For many people discouragement is the first stage in a multitude of emotionally crippling disorders. For others it serves as the catalyst for their theological pilgrimage—a pilgrimage that more often than not leads them to conclusions contrary to that of Scripture.

Discouragement is not part of God's plan for his children. To be free—and to remain free—from discouragement we must spiritually digest the promise in Galatians 6:9 to the point that it becomes a part of our thinking. To paraphrase the apostle Paul, it pays to do good. We may not see any immediate results from our good works, but the Scripture clearly teaches that God is taking notes (e.g., Mal. 3:14–16). At the proper time our faithfulness will be rewarded.

The tension centers around God's timing. We want results now. But in many cases God chooses to wait. The first step in

digging our way out of the pit of discouragement is to decide once and for all whether or not we are willing to live according to God's timetable. If not, discouragement will become a way of life. But once we entrust ourselves to his care—which of course includes his timing—we have hope; the one thing a discouraged man or woman has little or none of.

Are you discouraged? Does it seem that you are laboring in vain? Take a few moments to meditate on Galatians 6:9. Ask God to restore your confidence in him and his timetable for your life. And rest assured that you will in fact reap a good harvest, if you refuse to give up!

Heavenly Father, you are a God who rewards your faithful servants. You see and take note of all my labor. Thank you for the illustration of this that you have given us through your Son, who was greatly rewarded for his work on earth. Grant me the courage and endurance to keep on keeping on so that I may reap a reward at the proper time. Amen.

TOUCHSTONE

Persistence pays.

Do not be anxious about anything,
but in everything, by prayer and petition,
with thanksgiving, present your requests to God.

Philippians 4:6

Worry

There are places in Scripture where it appears that the writer is guilty of oversimplification. The way some topics are handled makes me wonder if the author has any idea of the type of world we live in. Paul's statement in Philippians 4:6 is one of those passages. How can he say, with such apparent flippancy, "Do not be anxious about anything"? Maybe you are tempted to respond to this verse the way I used to: "Paul, if you had my schedule, my financial obligations, and my responsibilities at home you would change your tune. Anybody who believes we should never worry has never really had anything to worry about."

As impractical as the advice in this verse may seem, there is one thing that brings me back to it again and again: Paul was in prison when he penned these words. Furthermore, Paul was a man consumed with a desire to take the Gospel of Christ all over the world. He was not somebody who enjoyed sitting around— much less sitting around chained to a Roman soldier. Yet in the midst of these far-less-than-ideal surroundings we find him admonishing the Christians in Philippi not to worry.

This brings us to some important questions: "What did Paul know that we don't know? How could he manage not to worry when his life and everything he had worked and lived for appeared to be in jeopardy?" He tells us in the second half of the verse: "But in everything, by prayer and petition, with thanksgiving, present your requests to God."

Paul trusted God completely. *He replaced worry with prayer, anxiety with faith.* He had a habit of remembering what we so easily forget—God is in control, and nothing takes him by surprise. God knew where Paul was. And he knew what Paul was and wasn't getting done. That was enough for the apostle. And the fact that he knows all about us must be enough for us as well.

What are you worried about? Try this: every time you begin to worry, pray instead. Tell the Lord what's going on and what

you feel needs to go on. Give him the details—your fears, your dreams, everything. Then tell him that unless he comes through, you are in trouble. In other words, put the burden on his shoulders. When you begin to worry again, repeat the process. After a couple of rounds of prayer you will begin experiencing peace. Long before your circumstances change, your feelings will change; you will sense a new internal freedom. Faith always brings freedom. What are you worrying about? Pray.

Heavenly Father, you are the God who knows my every care. You know the demands of this day. You are even aware of the added burdens tomorrow will bring. Remind me, Father, that you never intended for me to carry even one day's cares alone but that you have made yourself available to share and sometimes even bear my load. Remind me to pray rather than worry. Replace my anxiety with faith. Amen.

TOUCHSTONE

Replace worry with prayer,
and anxiety with faith.

Do nothing out of selfish ambition or vain conceit, but in humility consider others better than yourselves. Each of you should look not only to his own interests, but also to the interests of others. Your attitude should be the same as that of Christ Jesus.   Philippians 2:3–5

Controlling Conceit

No one enjoys being around individuals who are eaten up with themselves—men and women who are always talking about where *they* have been, who *they* know, and what *they* have accomplished. Although we can spot conceit in others a mile away, it is usually difficult to recognize it in ourselves. This is compounded by the fact that conceit takes on so many different forms. It's not only the loudmouth who can't stop talking about his or her last "big deal" who suffers from a case of conceit. Often it is the guy who never says a word—the one who is so absorbed in his own affairs that he can't be bothered by the concerns of others. The many disguises of conceit make each of us a vulnerable target.

In order to keep ourselves free from the web of conceit we must continually strive for humility. Maybe the idea of *striving for humility* sounds like a contradiction in terms. Perhaps, like many folks, you have always thought humility is just something some people are born with. Not so. Humility is something that is developed. In fact, we must all actively pursue humility or we will slowly gravitate toward some form of conceit.

So how do we free ourselves from conceit? How do we become humble? It is really very simple. Think of someone you admire, maybe someone you have admired from a distance but have never met. Choose someone who in the broad scheme of things you would consider *better* than you. Okay? How would you treat this individual if he or she were the next person you were to come into contact with? Now, make a decision to treat the next person you come into contact with the way you would the one you consider better than you. That is the *attitude* of humility. "But," you say, "what if I don't really believe the next person I come into contact with is better than I?" It doesn't matter! Just consider him to be better. That is the key to humility. It begins with an attitude.

There is one more thing. Make a decision to focus your next

conversation on the interests of the one you are talking with rather than your own. That is the *action* of humility. Ask questions. Listen attentively.

Jesus Christ did not die for you because you were actually worth dying for. He died for you because he *considered* you worth dying for. He put your best interests above his own—and he willingly marched to Calvary. Are you ready to be free from conceit? Then begin right now by preparing for your next encounter.

Lord Jesus, you are the One who deserves all honor, glory, and praise. Thank you for humbling yourself to the point of death in order to ensure my salvation. Remind me daily of your attitude and give me opportunities to demonstrate that same attitude toward others. Amen.

TOUCHSTONE

Consider others better, more worthy, and more honorable than yourself.

God said to him, "You fool!
This very night your life will be demanded from you.
Then who will get what you have prepared for
yourself?" Luke 12:20

Guarding Against Greed

I have never met a greedy man in my life. What I mean is that I have never met a person who would characterize himself or herself as greedy. Although greed is not a difficult term to define, it is terribly difficult to spot—in ourselves, that is. As one man put it, "The greedy man is the man who is more concerned about the accumulation of possessions than I am."

Greed creeps up on us. It begins with a sincere pursuit of fairness, a desire for our portion of the pie. Then somewhere along the way our campaign for fairness becomes a tool to justify irresponsible spending and accumulation. We defend our practice by reasoning that since it is *our* money we have the right to spend it as we please.

Jesus had some stern words for the greedy of his day. Take a minute and read Luke 12:13–34. No doubt the rich man in Jesus' parable was admired by those who knew him—just as we have a tendency to admire those who accumulate large fortunes today. But God called him a fool. "Now wait," we think; "maybe he was a little selfish, but a fool? How can a man who has the know-how to accumulate such incredible wealth be a fool?" Notice too that there is no mention of any wrongdoing on his part. Apparently he *earned* every penny of his massive estate. Yet God called him a fool. Why?

This man who was so wise in the things of this world was ignorant of the things of God. In his frenzy to accumulate wealth in this life he forgot about life in the hereafter. His mistake cost him dearly and eternally. Just as he was positioning himself for a life of ease, comfort, and pleasure, he lost it all. The very thing he refused to do willingly—give—he was ultimately forced to do.

Jesus went right to the heart of the matter when he said, "So is the man who lays up treasure for himself, and is not rich

toward God" (Luke 12:21). That is God's definition of greed: the pursuit of things here with little or no regard for the kingdom of God.

What percentage of your income do you invest in the kingdom of God? According to Jesus' definition, are you greedy? The truth that will set you free is this: on the day you die you will automatically give away all you own, but you will receive no credit for it in heaven. You have a choice. You can begin giving it away now—and have an unfailing treasure in heaven. Or you can continue to accumulate for yourself treasures on earth and have them taken from you by force. The choice is yours. The choice is clear.

> *Heavenly Father, you have set the precedent by giving your Son. Use this truth to revolutionize both my spending and my giving habits. I want to be rich toward you. Remind me to be on guard against greed. Give me discernment to catch it in its early stages and the courage to make whatever changes are necessary. Amen.*

TOUCHSTONE

Each of us will eventually give away all our earthly possessions. How we choose to do so, however, is a reflection of our commitment to the kingdom of God.

We must pay more careful attention,
therefore, to what we have heard,
so that we do not drift away. Hebrews 2:1

The Danger of Drifting

*D*uring the Second World War a battleship was anchored at the Azores off the coast of Spain. The sailors on watch asked a group of infantry men who happened to go on board, to stand watch while they went below for a meal. The soldiers were more than willing to help.

Unfortunately, they were untrained for their new responsibility. They were unaware that the ship's anchor was not secure and that the ship was gradually drifting toward shallow water. A trained seaman knows that he must periodically check a stationary landmark to keep tabs on the stability of a ship's anchorage. These eager soldiers, however, had not been taught what to watch for.

Within an hour the ship had drifted against a line of rocks. Minutes later a wave lifted the ship onto the rocks, ripping a hole in the bow. An alarm sounded, and the ship was evacuated. As the big cruiser heaved to one side, some equipment on deck collided and caught fire. Soon the entire vessel was engulfed in flames.

There is an unseen current that we all battle every day—a current that leads to certain destruction. We have all seen people drift away from God and the things of God. Oftentimes these are people we considered strong Christians.

Whenever I hear about something like that or see it happen, I always think about two things. First, everybody is susceptible; and I am certainly no exception. Second, I think about the warning in Hebrews 2:1. Here the author gives us the key to staying free from the effects of the tide that is constantly working to move us away from fellowship with the Father. "Pay attention!" he says. That is, "Direct your focus to the things pertaining to Christ and salvation." *We have a tendency to drift*

toward that on which we have focused our attention. This is why the Enemy is constantly working to get our attention—so he can influence our life's direction.

In light of how you spend your time and money, what is your focus? What are you paying close attention to during this time of your life? Has something or someone other than Christ captured your attention? If so, chances are you have begun to drift.

If the soldiers on deck had been paying attention to the shore in order to check the ship's movement, they could have avoided disaster. If you develop the habit of paying attention to a few reference points in your spiritual life, you too can avoid the eventual disaster that accompanies drifting.

Heavenly Father, thank you for this warning. Thank you for your concern. Give me keen insight into my own spiritual life so that I may catch myself in the initial stages of the process of drifting away from you. Make me a person whose focus is on Christ, and Christ alone. Amen.

TOUCHSTONE

The focus of our attention will determine our life's direction.

Every good and perfect gift is from above,
coming down from the Father of the heavenly lights. . .

James 1:17

A Grateful Heart

*T*he more I have, the more difficult it becomes to ward off ingratitude. As a child I was grateful for even the smallest blessing. My father died when I was only seven months old. My mother was left with almost nothing. By the time I was seventeen years old, I had lived in sixteen different houses in the same town. Gratitude came easy in those days. We were doing our best to survive. Every penny was counted and appreciated.

I guess one way to overcome an ungrateful spirit would be to lose everything. The old adage is true, you never know what you've got till it's gone. Anyone who has gone through a bankruptcy or been sued to the point of financial ruin can tell you all about that.

Other than by losing everything, how can we be free from ingratitude? Surely there is a way, for we are commanded to "give thanks in all circumstances" (1 Thess. 5:18).

To begin with, we must deal with an attitude that most of us adhere to in some form or another. It's an attitude that assumes we deserve the good life, that our hard work or perhaps the quality of our character has earned for us certain blessings and rewards. The truth, however, is that we deserve nothing. Why? Because sin separated us from the One who is the creator and bestower of all good things. It is only by the grace of God as expressed in Christ that we are allowed to participate in any good thing. Apart from God's love and concern for his prized creation there would be a vast chasm between us and all that is good in life.

There is no room for ingratitude in the life of a believer. For the truth is that *every* good gift is a grace gift from our heavenly Father. Why not take a few moments right now and thank him for the good things?

Heavenly Father, thank you for not giving me what I really deserve. I recognize that every good thing in my life is a grace gift from you. Guard me from the lie that somehow I deserve the good things in life. Remind me to express my gratitude daily—even for the smallest blessings. Thank you most of all for the gift of Jesus Christ. Amen.

TOUCHSTONE

Every good thing is from above.

Do not let this Book of the Law depart
  from your mouth;
meditate on it day and night, so that you may be careful
to do everything written in it.
Then you will be prosperous and successful.   Joshua 1:8

Free to Succeed

Next time you see a professional juggler, pay attention to where he focuses his attention. One would think a juggler would look at his hands, since that is where all the action is taking place. But a good juggler rarely looks down at his hands. He focuses on the point at which the objects he is juggling stop ascending and begin their descent. However, he does not watch any one object. He keeps his focus on the highest point.

Like the juggler, each of us has a number of things we must keep in motion—job, marriage, church, ministries, hobbies, children, education, etc. Our tendency is to begin focusing on one item to the neglect of others. We are deceived into believing that success in one area is an indication that we are successful, overall; when all the while we may be failing miserably in other departments. I have seen very talented women become so involved in social concerns that they fail in their responsibilities at home. We all know men whose financial accomplishments are the only measure of success they take seriously.

A juggler who could successfully juggle only one pin would not be considered much of a success. And a man or woman whose focus in life is any one area to the exclusion of the others is not much of a success either. Yet this is the situation in which many well-meaning believers find themselves.

The truth by which we can be set free from this dilemma is this: God will make you successful as you focus your attention on remaining faithful. God is committed to making you successful. The principles in his Word were given for that very purpose. But God takes a holistic approach. His goal is to grant you success in every area. He wants all your pins to stay airborne. The moment our focus becomes success rather than faithfulness, we begin working against God. At best we will be successfully juggling one pin while the others lie in disarray around us.

What is your focus, success or faithfulness? If it is difficult for you to imagine allowing God to prosper you at his pace

rather than your own and if the idea of shifting your focus away from success and onto faithfulness is a little threatening, think about the alternatives. Think about the price you are paying. Take a look at the lives of those who have traveled this road before you. Look at their health, their families, their reputation, their friends. Is it time you reevaluated the real meaning of success?

Father, you are the perfect picture of success. You keep all things perfectly balanced and in order. Give me the courage to turn my attention away from those things by which I tend to measure my success and to focus my eyes on you. Beginning today, I trust you to prosper me your way and according to your timetable.

TOUCHSTONE

Focus on faithfulness and trust God to make you successful.

Be still and know that I am God.   Psalm 46:10

A New Orientation

I am a textbook example of a goal-oriented, achievement-directed, bottom-line individual. Anyone who is like that or lives with someone like that knows both the positives and negatives associated with this kind of personality. One of the negatives is that it is difficult for me to slow down and relax. Even worse, sometimes it is difficult for me to pull away from my to-do list and focus on the One for whom I am supposedly to-doing!

There are several things that contribute to this problem. One is the value system of the world we live in. The world does not reward those whose character is beyond reproach. Neither does it recognize those who have a growing knowledge of God. Consequently, we are prone to begin measuring our success by the world's definition—visible achievement and progress. It should go without saying that there is nothing wrong with achievement and progress. However, when these things become our primary focus, it is only a matter of time until our private lives will begin to crumble from abuse and neglect.

I believe with all my heart that it is impossible to be both goal-oriented and God-oriented at the same time. One orientation will always take precedence over the other. Jesus said it this way: "No servant can serve two masters. Either he will hate the one and love the other, or he will be devoted to the one and despise the other" (Luke 16:13). When our desire to achieve takes the lead, several things happen in our relationship with God. He becomes a means to an end rather than the end. We tend to use God rather than worship him. We will find ourselves seeking *information about* him rather than *transformation by* him.

The question remains: How do we free ourselves from an unhealthy dose of goal orientation and become God-oriented? David summed it up beautifully: "Be still, and know that I am God." That is, *stop* whatever you are doing. Turn on the answering machine, turn down the volume, turn off the

television, put down the paper, close your door, and think. Item by item think about the things that absorb your time, emotion, and energy. Now measure their importance by this one single truth: "He is God."

So you have deadlines—He is God. Your kids are sick—He is God. Your boss is coming down hard on you—He is God. Your marriage is at an all-time low—He is God. David's point is simple. Take all that concerns you and measure it by this one overarching truth. And, suddenly, your focus shifts. Nothing is quite as monumental as you had thought. Circumstances are not quite as overwhelming. Things begin to settle into their proper perspective. After all, He is God.

This renewal of perspective is not a quarterly review of your life. There are days when it needs to be an hourly exercise. Regardless of your circumstances, take time every day to stop and reflect on all of life's demands in light of the One who sovereignly and lovingly watches over you at all times.

Heavenly Father, you are the God who never sleeps or slumbers. You are the Master of all creation. You are the standard by which all things are measured. Remind me to approach all of life mindful of the fact that you are God. Amen.

TOUCHSTONE

It is impossible to be both goal-oriented and God-oriented at the same time.

For even the Son of Man did not come to be served,
but to serve, and to give his life as a ransom for many.

Mark 10:45

The Service Syndrome

*W*e live in a service-oriented society. Every year the demand for services increases. You can hire someone to do just about anything. Businesses designed to meet this growing demand are cropping up everywhere. Nowadays you can have just about any type of food brought to your home. Catalog companies have made it possible to purchase everything from clothes to camping gear by phone. You can even punch a few keys on your PC and have your groceries delivered right to your front door.

All of us enjoy being served. Isn't it true that a significant portion of our personal budgets go toward paying for services: water, electricity, housekeeping, babysitting, lawn care, interest payments, car repair, etc.? Many of these services are luxuries we have grown so accustomed to having that we consider them necessities.

With so much available to us we are set up to believe a lie that has been around since Jesus' day. Simply put, it is this: *Those who are served the most, are the most important.* Or, the greatest of all are served by all. We need to learn on a spiritual level what many businesses are learning on a monetary level. It is really those who do the serving who reap the most benefit. In this world, the businesses that can offer the greatest number of services to their customers will win the lion's share of the market; they will reap the greatest reward. Similarly, the believer who is the greatest servant in this life will reap the greatest reward in the life to come.

We are rulers in training. To be great later on in God's kingdom, you and I must be servants now. This runs against our grain for two reasons. First of all because the world has modeled the opposite for us all our lives. And second, our sinful flesh is constantly crying out for recognition and service. Regardless of the resistance we face, however, we would be wise to begin

practicing servanthood today; it is the key to greatness in the kingdom to come.

As you think through the day ahead, who are the people you normally expect to serve you? How could you serve them instead? "For even the Son of Man did not come to be served, but to serve, and to give his life as a ransom for many."

Heavenly Father, you are the God who deserves all my service and yet humbled yourself to serve me through Christ. Thank you for the example I have in your Son. Remind me throughout the day that you have left me here as a servant. Through my consistent service draw others to yourself. Amen.

TOUCHSTONE

Those who serve in this life will rule in the world to come.

Then he said to them all:
"If anyone would come after me,
he must deny himself
and take up his cross daily and follow me."

Luke 9:23

The Risk of Surrender

*T*o the nonbeliever the idea of unconditionally surrendering oneself to a God no one can see sounds ludicrous. Understandably so. But even to many seasoned Christians the notion of surrender is somewhat threatening. Something on the inside of each of us shrinks back at the thought of abandoning ourselves to do God's bidding. As much as we enjoy singing about his sacrifice for us, the thought of returning the favor—unconditionally—makes us a little antsy.

When Jesus spoke of denying ourselves he was not thinking of some sort of monastic existence. Jesus did not live his life hidden away from the world. To deny ourselves is to simply say no to our desires when they conflict with God's will. Jesus made it clear that he did not have a single act in mind. He was calling for a lifestyle of denial. In another words, *sacrifice*.

Maybe the very thought of such a thing makes you shudder. You are not alone. Churches are full of people who need to be set free from their fear of sacrifice. And there is a simple truth that will do just that.

In the verses that follow today's passage Jesus mentions three things that will take place in the lives of those who refuse to follow him. In essence he is saying, "I understand what you are feeling. I understand your fear of the unknown. But take a good look at the alternatives, and you will understand why following me is the wisest choice you could make."

What are the alternatives? First of all, the people who can't find it within themselves to live for Christ will eventually lose everything they have lived for anyway. There will be nothing of eternal value to show for their lives. It's true, you can't take it with you. Second, those who see sacrifice for Christ as a threat to their security will eventually lose everything they thought made them secure to begin with. In essence, they will lose themselves. And last, refusing to surrender to the lordship of Christ results in the forfeiting of eternal status and recognition. Jesus put it this

way: "If anyone is ashamed of me and my words, the Son of Man will be ashamed of him when he comes in his glory and in the glory of the Father" (Luke 9:26).

When you think about it, the man or woman who refuses to surrender to the will of God is really the one making the greatest sacrifice. Jim Elliott had it right when he said, "He is no fool who gives what he cannot keep to gain what he cannot lose." Have you been holding out on God? What is it that he wants from you? In light of eternity, is it really that much of a sacrifice? In light of eternity, is it really a sacrifice at all?

Heavenly Father, thank you for sacrificing what was most precious to you in order to make it possible for me to know you. Give me eyes to see past the temporal and into the eternal. Remind me to measure every supposed sacrifice by the standard you set at Calvary and by the certainty of eternity. You have shown the way. I pray for wisdom and courage to follow.

TOUCHSTONE

If you think the cost of discipleship is high, consider the price paid by those who refuse to be his disciples.

Therefore everyone who hears these words of mine and puts them into practice is like a wise man who built his house on the rock. Matthew 7:24

Taking the Long Look

*I*n an address to the 1984 United States Olympic team, President Reagan made this comment: "You above all people know that it is not just the will to win that counts, but the will to prepare to win." Wherever there is the potential for great gain, there is usually the necessity for equal or greater sacrifice. Those who have excelled in their professions understand the relationship between accomplishment and sacrifice. Many believers are unaware of the fact that this same principle applies in the spiritual realm as well.

Jesus chose to communicate this important truth in a parable. Two men decided to build houses. One decided to take the easy way. He built his house on a river bank where the foundation would be easy to put in and materials were readily available. The other man chose the difficult task of hauling all his building supplies up to the top of a mountain. Once there, it took him days just to put in a foundation.

From the outset of the parable Jesus makes it clear who these two men represent. The first man represents that group of people who find the teachings of Christ too restrictive, too difficult to obey. The other builder represents those who are willing to pay the price of obedience. They are the few who are willing to put into "practice" what Jesus taught.

For a while it looked as if the man on the mountain had worked extra hard for nothing. But then the clouds began to gather. And soon the wind began to blow. Before long both houses were being battered by the wind. It was then that the man on the mountain began to fully enjoy the benefits of his hard labor. At the same time, his friend down below was probably thinking, "If only I had. . . ." But it was too late. And so it goes with those who cannot bring themselves to pay the price of obedience to Christ.

For many, freedom from sin involves pausing long enough to take the long look. What is it about Christ's teachings that you

find too difficult to practice? No doubt you have the will to *endure* the storms of life. But willpower isn't enough. The real issue is, do you have the will *to prepare* for life's storms? Jesus was clear: obedience now ensures endurance later.

Heavenly Father, when obedience becomes difficult, remind me to take the long look. Bring to my mind the people in my life who are reaping the blessings of their decision to obey you when it wasn't convenient. Thank you for giving us principles that make for an enduring foundation. Use this truth to set me free from my spiritual nearsightedness. As I face life's storms, sustain me in such a way that others will be drawn to you. Amen.

TOUCHSTONE

Obedience to Christ enables us to endure the storms of life.

Take my yoke upon you and learn from me,
for I am gentle and humble in heart,
and you will find rest for your souls. Matthew 11:29

The Yoke of Freedom

Generally speaking, we do not associate freedom with a yoke. The two concepts strike us as opposites. And yet the very one who said he came to set us free also invited us to share his yoke. Hmm. To complicate matters even further he promised *rest* for those who take him up on his offer. Once again we are confronted with what seems to be a contradiction in terms. How can one possibly find rest by putting on a yoke?

When Jesus spoke of a yoke, he was referring to a relationship—a relationship in which two would walk side by side in the same direction, covering the same ground, encountering the same obstacles, traveling at the same speed. By inviting his audience to submit to his yoke, he was asking them to come alongside him. In essence he was offering three things. First, he was offering to help shoulder their burden. Second, he was offering to guide them, for whenever two oxen were yoked together, one was always considered the lead animal. And third, Jesus was offering to instruct them in the ways of freedom.

The Savior knows how to keep your marriage free from the destructive forces prevalent in our society. He knows how to free your mind from jealousy, greed, and lust. He knows how to help you avoid becoming enslaved to destructive habits and attitudes. And so he invites you to come alongside him and learn the ways of freedom. He offers you an opportunity to walk beside him through the maze of attitudes, opportunities, and relationships that would threaten your liberty.

Many view the yoke of Christ as a threat to freedom. From their perspective a yoke is a yoke regardless of who it belongs to. It was for this very reason that Christ made his offer to the "weary and burdened" (Matt. 11:28)—those who had tried to find freedom on their own and had found only bondage instead. To those he said, "Come to me . . . and I will give you rest."

Has your quest for freedom led you to despair? Are you ready to come alongside the only One who can truly set you free?

Christ came that we might *experience* freedom, not just wish for it. Yet it is only when we humble ourselves and team up with him that personal freedom becomes a reality.

Heavenly Father, thank you for allowing me the privilege of intimacy with your Son. Thank you for the promise of rest and freedom. I willingly surrender myself to the teaching and instruction of the Lord Jesus. Give me ears to hear his voice and eyes to see his path. Lead me into freedom. Amen.

TOUCHSTONE

*By submitting ourselves to the
yoke of Christ today, we
ensure for ourselves the
freedom of Christ tomorrow.*

It is for freedom that Christ has set us free.
Stand firm, then, and do not let yourselves
be burdened again by a yoke of slavery.

Galatians 5:1

Standing Firm

As Americans we have been blessed with a great deal of freedom. But our freedom was not without cost. Thousands of men and women sacrificed their lives to guarantee it. And thousands more are willing to do the same in order to maintain this valuable commodity. As long as there are forces in this world bent on stealing our freedom, there is the necessity of having men and women who focus on its preservation. So then, in the process of enjoying our freedom, we are constantly having to guard against those who would take it away.

The same principle holds true in the spiritual realm. Our independence from the domination of sin with all its trappings carried a high price tag. It cost God a great deal—his Son. Yet the battle for freedom did not end at Calvary. For it is only as we discover the truth and appropriate it that the liberty made available at the cross becomes a reality in our lives. But even then our struggle is not over. For there are forces all around us working to undermine our freedom. Whispers of condemnation, feelings of fear and insecurity, graceless messages from well-meaning pastors, constant criticism from those we love. Day after day our freedom is assailed from all sides.

It was this very threat that moved the apostle Paul to write, "Stand firm, then, and do not let yourselves be burdened again by a yoke of slavery." He knew from watching the Christians in Galatia that a believer's freedom must be constantly defended. For just as the truth can set us free, so the lies of the enemy can send us right back to the bondage we once knew.

Maintaining our spiritual freedom is much like defending our national freedom. In both cases we must guard against those who would rob us of our liberties. And in both cases the struggle is well worth the effort. What about you? Are you standing firm in the freedom Christ provided at the cross? Are you appropriating that truth daily? If not, take a few minutes to review the areas in which you know God wants to set you free. Today begin

memorizing and meditating on the specific truths that apply to your situation. It was so you could experience freedom that Christ even bothered to set you free. Isn't it time you took him up on his offer?

Heavenly Father, thank you for sending Christ to pave the way for my freedom. Give me the wisdom to know how to protect this precious and costly gift. When I am bombarded by the lies intended to rob me of my Christian liberty, bring to my mind those truths that have proved themselves so effective against the weapons of our enemy. Use my freedom to draw others to yourself. And grant me the grace to continue standing firm. Amen.

TOUCHSTONE

*Christ died to make us free;
let us honor him by
refusing to settle for
anything less.*